I0098702

Published by Julie Ginos

Text copyright© 2014 Julie Ginos
Illustrations copyright© 2014 Jimmy Trapp
First Printing, September 2014
ISBN 978-0692289303

All rights reserved. No part of this publication may be reproduced or transmitted in any
form or by any means, electronic or mechanical, including photocopy, recording, or any
information storage and retrieval system, without written permission from Julie Ginos.

For Gavin, Evelyn, Avril &
especially Oliver.
May you always let Daddy
tickle you!

With Love,

Mommy

Special Thanks and Acknowledgements to

The Bennett Family
Brandon and Mitzi Buckman Family
Norman and Debby Kendrick
Tony & Luie

Oliver brushes his teeth and says his prayers
every night when it's time for bed.

Tonight he is wearing his blue pajamas
with buttons and stripes of red.

Daddy comes in to say "Good Night."
But Oliver knows his plan.

Daddy tucks him in tight, and leans in close
and raises his tickle hands.

The giggling starts right away
and lasts for quite a while.

"Hmm," he thinks, "maybe tomorrow
I should try a different style."

The very next day, Oliver thinks and thinks
about which pajamas to choose.

Maybe he should try the ones with feet.
They make it like wearing shoes!

So he brushes his teeth, and says his prayers
and climbs into his bed.

Tonight he's wearing his footie jammies,
thinking they might work instead!

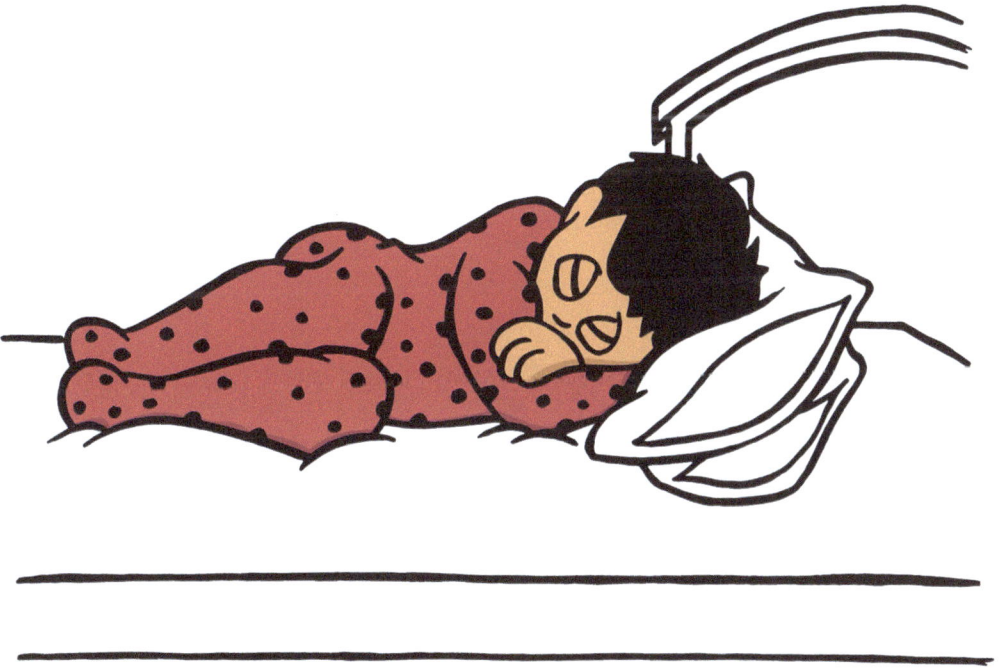

In comes Daddy to say, "Good Night."
Again, Oliver knows his plan.

He tucks him in tight, and leans in close
and raises his tickle hands!

To Oliver's surprise, the footie pajamas
don't help a single bit!

Daddy's tickles throw him straight into
a super-giggling fit!

So the next night comes and Oliver thinks,
"I must get prepared!"

"Which pajamas of mine do I wear
to help my ribs be spared?"

"A-HA!" he says, "I've got just the ones
that will most definitely keep me safe!"

My superhero pajamas *always* work!
And I even have my cape!

So in comes Daddy to say, "Good Night."
As always, Oliver knows his plan.

Daddy tucks him in tight, and leans in close
and raises his tickle hands.

As every night, just like before,
Daddy's tickles make Oliver giggle.

Oliver squirms and screams and moves around,
and even starts to wiggle.

But this time Oliver realizes,
every other night just like this one,

He actually likes when Daddy tickles him,
it really is lots of fun!

About the Author

Julie Ginos is a mom of three, almost four amazing kids: Gavin, Oliver, Evelyn & Avril. She has been married to Alex for eight years and their life is centered around artistic creativity, whether it's writing a children's book, making music with her husband and children, planning awesome birthday parties, or working as a photographer. She hopes this title, "Oliver and the Tickle-Proof Pajamas" is the first of many children's books to come that will delightfully engage many young children all while sharing a little of what she gets to witness and be a part of daily as a mom. The Ginos family resides in Quincy, IL, where they enjoy being close with family and friends.

You can contact Julie anytime at juliahkendrick@yahoo.com or visit her photography site at http://www.gsphotography.zenfolio.com.

About the Illustrator

Jimmy Trapp is an illustrator in Fort Collins, CO, who specializes in the weird and zaney. He often times wonders if he ever grew up, but quickly reminds himself that, despite having to do adult things, he's still a kid at heart. Jimmy has dreams of writing and drawing his own graphic novel, as well as opening a coffee shop where artists from all types of genres can display their artwork for the world to see. It's also an excuse to nerd-out with other fellow artists who like superheroes, giant robots, ninjas, martians, talking apes, and wizards.

More of his work can be found at https://www.facebook.com/pencilscoffeeandmarkers or http://morningcoffeecupart.tumblr.com.
You can also contact him at jimmyqtrapp@gmail.com.

Special thanks to Vaughn Donahue for providing his talents as colorist. Vaughn is a graphic and web designer and can be contacted through his website, www.destinationgraphic.com

www.ingramcontent.com/pod-product-compliance
Lightning Source LLC
Chambersburg PA
CBHW041800040426
42447CB00001B/33